Seasons

Summer

Siân Smith

www.heinemannlibrary.co.uk

Visit our website to find out more information about Heinemann Library books.

To order:

☎ Phone +44 (0) 1865 888066

📄 Fax +44 (0) 1865 314091

💻 Visit www.heinemannlibrary.co.uk

Heinemann Library is an imprint of Capstone Global Library Limited, a company incorporated in England and Wales having its registered office at 7 Pilgrim Street, London, EC4V 6LB – Registered company number: 6695582

Heinemann is a registered trademark of Pearson Education Limited, under licence to Capstone Global Library Limited

Edited by Rebecca Rissman, Charlotte Guillain, and Siân Smith
Designed by Joanna Hinton-Malivoire
Picture research by Elizabeth Alexander and Sally Claxton
Production by Duncan Gilbert
Originated by Heinemann Library
Printed and bound in China by South China Printing Company Ltd

ISBN 978 0 431 19279 6
13 12 11 10 09
10 9 8 7 6 5 4 3 2 1

British Library Cataloguing in Publication Data

Smith, Siân
 Summer. - (Seasons)
 1. Summer - Juvenile literature
 I. Title
 508.2

Acknowledgements

The author and publisher are grateful to the following for permission to reproduce copyright material: ©Alamy pp.**15** (Alex Segre), **19** (Arco Images GmbH), **14** (Blend Images), **13** (Bubbles Photolibrary), **18** (Image Source Black), **21** (Imagestate), **20** (Jon Arnold Images Ltd.), **12** (Jupiter Images/Thinkstock), **8** (Nick Baylis), **11**, **23 bottom** (Romain Bayle), **9** (Simone van den Berg); ©Capstone Global Library Ltd. p.**16** (2005/Malcolm Harris); ©Corbis pp.**04 br** (Image100), **04 tl** (Zefa/Roman Flury); ©Digital Vision p.**17** (Rob van Petten); ©Getty Images pp.**10** (Ariel Skelley), **04 tr** (Floria Werner), **7** (IIC/ Axiom), **5** (Kazuo Ogawa/Sebun Photo); ©iStockphoto pp.**6**, **23 top** (Bojan Tezak), **04 bl** (Inga Ivanova), **22** (Tatiana Grozetskaya).

Cover photograph of a meadow reproduced with permission of ©Shutterstock (Katerina Havelkova). Back cover photograph reproduced with permission of ©Digital Vision (Rob Van Patten).

Every effort has been made to contact copyright holders of material reproduced in this book. Any omissions will be rectified in subsequent printings if notice is given to the publishers.

Contents

What is summer?

spring

summer

autumn

winter

There are four seasons every year.

4

Summer is one of the four seasons.

When is summer?

spring

summer

winter

autumn

The four seasons follow a pattern.

Summer comes after spring.

The weather in summer

It can be sunny in summer.

8

It can be hot in summer.

What can we see in summer?

In summer we can see people wearing t-shirts.

10

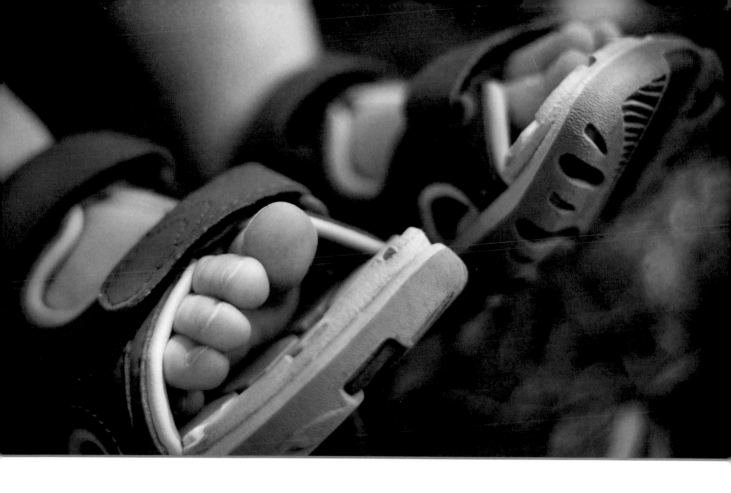

In summer we can see people wearing sandals.

In summer we can see people wearing hats.

In summer we can see people putting on sun cream.

In summer we can see people watering plants.

14

In summer we can see people swimming.

In summer we can see people
on holiday.

In summer we can see people
having picnics.

In summer we can see people
eating ice cream.

In summer we can see fruit.

In summer we can see flowers.

In summer we can see bees.

21

Which season comes next?

Which season comes after summer?

22

Picture glossary

pattern happening in the same order

sandal type of shoe with an open top

Index

Notes for parents and teachers

Before reading

Listen to a few minutes of *Summer* from Vivaldi's *Four Seasons*. Tell the children to close their eyes and think about the following images of summer: building sandcastles, feeling the warm sun, eating ice cream, playing in a paddling pool. Talk to the children about the different things they do in summer. What sort of clothes do they wear? Do they eat any different foods? Do they like the summer more than any of the other seasons?

After reading

• Make summer flowers. You will need: coloured paper, scissors, pencil/crayons, straws, sticky tape. Tell the children to choose a sheet of paper of any colour they like for their flower. Tell them to draw round their hand as many times as possible to fit on the paper. Cut out the hands. Then pinch all the bases of the hands together and fix with sticky tape onto the straw. Separate out the petals (fingers) by pulling gently away from the centre. They should cut leaves out of green paper and attach them to the stem (straw).

• Memory game. Place pictures of items associated with summer onto a tray. For example: a sun, sandcastle, ice-cream, strawberry, sunglasses, sun hat. Tell the children to look at the objects for 20 seconds. Then turn away from the children and remove one of the pictures. Turn back and ask the children what is missing.

• Music and movement. Play some more of Vivaldi's *Four Seasons, Summer*. Tell the children to imagine that they are going on a trip to the seaside. They will mime what is happening: getting into the car, driving to the beach, playing on the sand, searching in the rock pools, going swimming in the sea, having a picnic, and then driving home.